LETTER TO UNDERSTAND THE TRUTH

FOR MY HUSBAND

COVER / PICTURES /
AUTHOR

TANJA FEILER

DEAR SIR OR MADAM,

I'M BUILT BY PROFESSIONAL THERAPIST (7 YEARS IN THE PSYCHIATRY 10 THERAPY GROUPS FORMED 60 CLIENTS AND 50 ERGOTHERAPIEPRAKTIKATINNEN. I WAS IN THE BR AND GOT MY TRAINING WITH VERY GOOD CUT. TRAINING IPT WAF PARTICIPATED

PSYCHOEDUCATION, SO I'M STILL BEHAVIORAL THERAPIST ... AND BEFOR I EVER MY EDUCATION FROM 1996 – DID IN 1999, I HAVE WORKED FOR TWO YEARS IIM CULTURE AREA OF NEWSPAPER AND BY THE END OF 1995 IN RENO (SHOES MOLD, REPACK) BONE WORK, AS THE PRECONDITION FOR GRANT FOR TRAINING AS THAT IS 70 PERCENT . EXPERIENCE I HAVE WHILE WORKING IN THE RENO FERNKUSE IN

PHILOSOPHY AND PSYCHOLOGY AT THE UNIVERSITY OF HAGEN HAS TO MENTALLY NOT STARVE FINALLY, I KNEW THAT I DID NOT JAHRZENTELANG IN RENO STAY –.. BUT I CREATE A BASE I WAS 300 TAKEN CANDIDATES. I FOUGHT FOR TRAINING AND WANTED VERY WELL MADE. A CLASSMATE WHO WAS ALMOST FINISHED WITH HER STUDIES AS A DOCTOR, SHE HAD IN OPHTHALMOLOGIST AREA IT WITH. THEN THEY

THREW IN THE STUDY TO BE ERGOTHEAPEUTIN. SHE HAS TRAINING WITH THE MARK OF 4 AND PLANNED TO SUE THE SCHOOL. SHE HAS THREE YEARS ESPECIALLY IN THE SUBJECTS OF ANATOMY LECTURER CORRECTIONS LESSONS TROTDEM WE WERE FRIENDS. I HAVE ESTABLISHED A STUDY GROUP, AND AS WE HAVE LEARNED TOGETHER WEEKLY ONCE PSYCHOLOGY THE WEEK

AFTER OCCUPATIONAL MEDICINE ... THE STUDENT WHO SAT NEXT TO ME, HAD NO IDEA OF PSYCHOLOGY. I TOLD HER EVERYTHING ...

FINANCED I HAVE (PAY 70% SUBSIDY, REST 30 PERCENT SELF) TRAINING AND HAVE AS A FREELANCER IN THE CULTURAL SECTOR PROGRESS– (OWN SERIES) INTERVIEWS WITH CELEBRITIES AMONG

OTHERS HORST JANSON .... THAT IS, I HAD CA SIX APPOINTMENTS IN THE EVENINGS AND HAVE THE ARTICLE WRITTEN AT NIGHT AND LEARNED. ANYWAY, I HAVE A DAY AFTER TRAINING DIRECTLY IN THE SOCIAL PSYCH. STARTING FROM THE BEGINNING AND HAD MY OWN AREA. THAT WAS IN 1999. IN 2000, I WENT THROUGH A MUTUAL FRIEND OF WITH AND MY HUSBAND (I AM MY HUSBAND BUT NEVER MET)

RECEIVED A MANUSCRIPT. WE CHILDREN OF THE WORLD BY DIRK L. FEILER. THE MANUSCRIPT HAS MY HUSBAND IN TOWN VK BECAUSE I LIVED UP TO MY 17TH YEAR OF LIFE, THEN KAISERSLAUTERN, DISTRIBUTED TO OBTAIN REVIEWS AMONG OTHERS BY DR. BÄUML, A RENOWNED PERSONALITY I HAVE COME TO KNOW AS PART OF A TRAINING , MY HUSBAND'S MANUSCRIPT IS FANTASTIC, I HAVE MADE IT

REQUIRED READING FOR MY INTERNS, THE PSYHOLOGE THE DEVICE, THE SECOND BOSS, WAS VERY EXCITED. HE SAID THAT WAS SOMETHING ELSE ENTIRELY HIS COMMENT IS THE BEST. I WANTED THE AUTHOR ALWAYS KNOW AND SUDDENLY ON 17/3/2002 I WAS INVITED BY A FRIEND SAID, I WAS FOR THE FIRST TIME EVER IN HIS HOME, AND HE SAID IT'LL STILL GAST.DA EVENING I WANTED WITH MY

FORMER CIRCLE OF FRIENDS
TO MEET, I HAD TO 7:30
ALREADY HIT BY VK TO KL,
BUT WE ENTERTAINED
THREE HOURS. WHILE
DRIVING, THE FLASH IS
STAMPED, I KNEW HIM WILL
YOU MARRY SIX MONTHS
LATER, WE DID WELL, HALF
A YEAR LATER
ECCLESIASTICAL, 2011, WE
HAVE OUR MARRIAGE VOWS
RENEWED (I KNOW FROM AN
AMERICAN SERIES). IN
2005 MY HUSBAND HAS
PUBLISHED HIS BOOK AND

IT HAS MADE ITS WAY IN THE WORLD. BEFORE I MET MY HUSBAND I WAS SOME TIME BEFORE 4 YEARS IN A RELATIONSHIP THAT HAS RUINED ME FINANCIALLY. € 20,000 DEBT BY THIS MAN WHO INSPIRED BY MY THERAPIST OCCUPATION TRAINING AS A HEALING EDUCATOR BEGAN IN HEIDELBERG (HE'S COOKING WAS), BUT FOR HEALTH REASONS HE COULD NO LONGER WORK AS A COOK. I HELPED HIM OF COURSE,

AND HE HAS BROKEN WITH
HAS TAKEN HIS MEDICATION
AND LIGHTER COLLECTION
AND WE ARRANGED TO
MEET LATER FOR THE
WEEK, SO THAT HE GETS
HIS CLOTHES ETC. THEN
END 2,001TH BUT WHEN I
CAME ON THE DAY AT 18
O'CLOCK HOME, THE
APARTMENT WAS VACATED
HALF EMPTY. MY HUSBAND
HAS RESTORED ME
FINANCIALLY, HE CLARIFIED
EVERYTHING AND
EVERYTHING WAS O.K. SO

CREDIT CARD WE HAD A LOT OF MONEY, THREE MONTHS AFTER THE DEPARTURE OF PATRICK HAVE PATRICK AND I TELEPHONED. WE HAD AT THAT TIME OF THE CONTRACT 02 FOR COUPLES AND I HAD TELEFNIERT 300 EUROS, WHICH HE WANTED TO SUE. AND HE SAID HE WILL BECOME A FATHER, HE HAS CHEATED DURING HIS TRAINING. THEN SHORT RELATIONS AND HAB BEGINNING OF MARCH

2002 A VERY ATTRACTIVE LARGE MAN KNOW LEARNED WHO ADORED ME. HE WANTED TO INTRODUCE ME TO HIS MOTHER EASTER, BECAUSE I'M A THERAPIST, I COULD MAYBE HELP YOU. THEN I MET DIRK AND MADE A FEW DAYS LATER BY TELEPHONE CIRCUIT. WHEN MY HUSBAND AND I FIRST MET, WE HAVE BEGUN TO LAUNCH SOCIAL PROJECTS HERE IN KL, THERE IS NO DAYCARE FOR PSYCH. ILL, FOR OVER 10 YEARS, WE

ARE COMMITTED, STILL. THEN UP STARTED COUNSELING, WE WERE LIVING IN A RETAIL STORE AND HAVE IN THE SHOP WINDOW A STAND, WE HAVE MADE YOURSELF: WRITE A BOOK. AND OUT OF NOWHERE CAME TO WRITE A MAN WHO WAS THEREFORE MOTIVATED .... THEN I WAS MADE REDUNDANT PROFESSIONALLY AND FELL INTO DEPRESSION, AM SINCE 2013 DISABILITY ALLOWANCE WRITE BOOKS.

MEANWHILE, MY HUSBAND AND I 500 PUBLISHED IN THE INTERNATIONAL BOOK MARKET. FOR TWO YEARS, I FOCUS ON CHILDREN'S BOOKS. THE CUTE PETS.

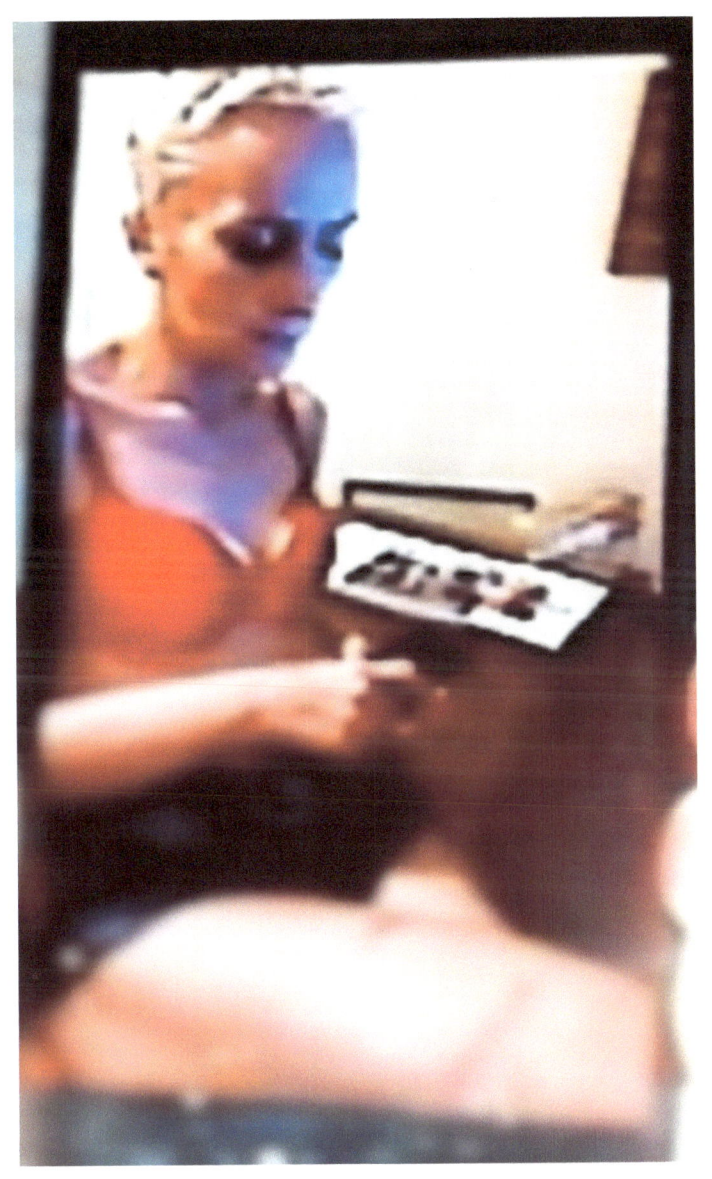

22

I ESPECIALLY THANK MY
HUSBAND

www.ingramcontent.com/pod-product-compliance
Lightning Source LLC
Chambersburg PA
CBHW050931290526
45792CB00002B/977